PLAN AND PREPARE!

By CHARLES GHIGNA

Illustrations by GLENN THOMAS

Music by DREW TEMPERANTE

CANTATA
LEARNING

WWW.CANTATALEARNING.COM

CANTATA LEARNING

Published by Cantata Learning
1710 Roe Crest Drive
North Mankato, MN 56003
www.cantatalearning.com

Library of Congress Cataloging-in-Publication Data
Names: Ghigna, Charles. | Thomas, Glenn, illustrator. | Temperante, Drew.
Title: Plan and prepare! / by Charles Ghigna ; illustrations by Glenn Thomas
 ; music by Drew Temperante.
Description: North Mankato, MN : Cantata Learning, [2018] | Series: Fire
 safety | Audience: Age 3-8. | Audience: K to grade 3.
Identifiers: LCCN 2017007566 (print) | LCCN 2017017826 (ebook) | ISBN
 9781684100460 | ISBN 9781684100453 (hardcover : alk. paper) | ISBN
 9781684100743 (pbk. : alk. paper)
Subjects: LCSH: Dwellings--Fires and fire prevention--Juvenile literature. |
 Fires--Safety measures--Juvenile literature.
Classification: LCC TH9445.D9 (ebook) | LCC TH9445.D9 G455 2018 (print) | DDC
 628.9/22--dc23
LC record available at https://lccn.loc.gov/2017007566

Book design, Tim Palin Creative
Editorial direction, Flat Sole Studio
Executive musical production and direction, Elizabeth Draper
Music arranged and produced by Drew Temperante

ACCESS THE MUSIC!

SCAN CODE WITH MOBILE APP

CANTATALEARNING.COM

Printed in the United States   4995

TIPS TO SUPPORT LITERACY AT HOME

WHY READING AND SINGING WITH YOUR CHILD IS SO IMPORTANT

Daily reading with your child leads to increased academic achievement. Music and songs, specifically rhyming songs, are a fun and easy way to build early literacy and language development. Music skills correlate significantly with both phonological awareness and reading development. Singing helps build vocabulary and speech development. And reading and appreciating music together is a wonderful way to strengthen your relationship.

READ AND SING EVERY DAY!

TIPS FOR USING CANTATA LEARNING BOOKS AND SONGS DURING YOUR DAILY STORY TIME

1. As you sing and read, point out the different words on the page that rhyme. Suggest other words that rhyme.

2. Memorize simple rhymes such as Itsy Bitsy Spider and sing them together. This encourages comprehension skills and early literacy skills.

3. Use the questions in the back of each book to guide your singing and storytelling.

4. Read the included sheet music with your child while you listen to the song. How do the music notes correlate to the words of the song?

5. Sing along on the go and at home. Access music by scanning the QR code on each Cantata book. You can also stream or download the music for free to your computer, smartphone, or mobile device.

Devoting time to daily reading shows that you are available for your child. Together, you are building language, literacy, and listening skills.

Have fun reading and singing!

Fire **safety** starts with you! If there is a fire in your home, what should you do? You will know if you have an escape plan. Prepare for an emergency by practicing this plan with your family.

Now turn the page to **practice** these important fire safety skills. Remember to sing along!

Fire safety starts with you,
when you know just what to do.

Rule One! Have a plan!

Talk to your family.
Make a plan to meet.
Practice getting out.
It's the fire safety beat!

Make a plan and practice.
Stay **calm** and cool.
Know where to meet.
Use the safety rules!

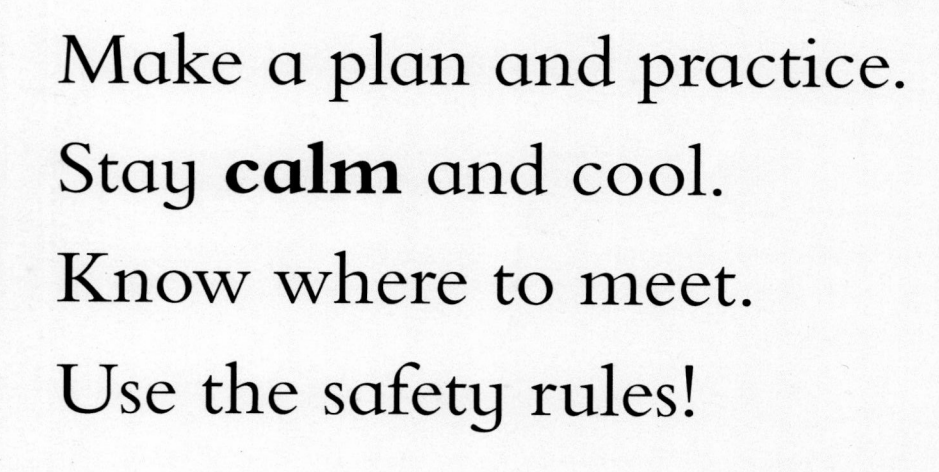

Rule Two! Get out fast!

You should never stay.
You should never hide.
Get out. Get out fast.
Get yourself outside.

Make a plan and practice.
Stay calm and cool.
Know where to meet.
Use the safety rules!

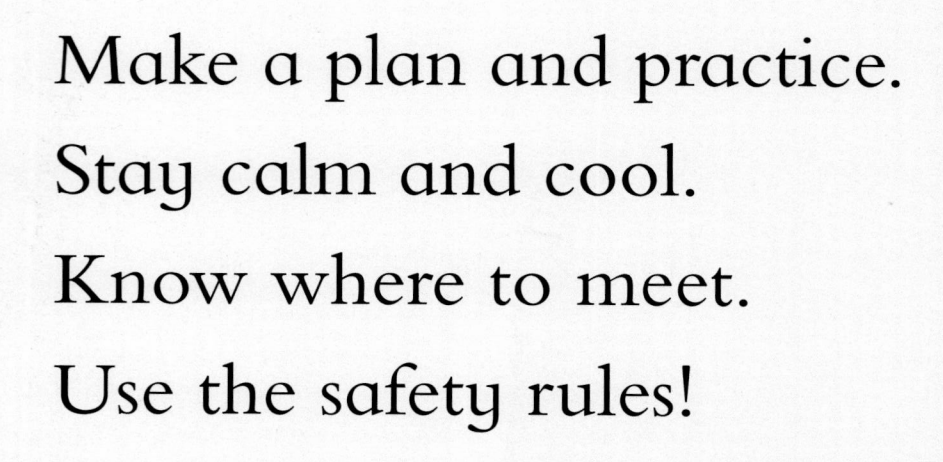

Rule Three! Stay low!

If there is thick smoke,
practice what you know.
Get down. Crawl out fast.
Get yourself down low.

Make a plan and practice.

Stay calm and cool.

Know where to meet.

Use the safety rules!

Rule Four! Don't open hot doors!

Find another way out
if a door feels hot.
Do not open it.

If it's hot, do not!

Make a plan and practice.
Stay calm and cool.
Know where to meet.
Use the safety rules!

Fire safety starts with you,
when you know just what to do.

SONG LYRICS
Plan and Prepare

Fire safety starts with you,
when you know just what to do.

Rule One! Have a plan!
Talk to your family.
Make a plan to meet.
Practice getting out.
It's the fire safety beat!

Make a plan and practice.
Stay calm and cool.
Know where to meet.
Use the safety rules!

Rule Two! Get out fast!
You should never stay.
You should never hide.
Get out. Get out fast.
Get yourself outside.

Make a plan and practice.
Stay calm and cool.
Know where to meet.
Use the safety rules!

Rule Three! Stay low!
If there is thick smoke,
practice what you know.
Get down. Crawl out fast.
Get yourself down low.

Make a plan and practice.
Stay calm and cool.
Know where to meet.
Use the safety rules!

Rule Four! Don't open hot doors!
Find another way out
if a door feels hot.
Do not open it.
If it's hot, do not!

Make a plan and practice.
Stay calm and cool.
Know where to meet.
Use the safety rules!

Fire safety starts with you,
when you know just what to do.

Plan and Prepare

Hip Hop
Drew Temperante

Verse 2
Rule Two! Get out fast!
You should never stay.
You should never hide.
Get out. Get out fast.
Get yourself outside.

Chorus

Verse 3
Rule Three! Stay low!
If there is thick smoke,
practice what you know.
Get down. Crawl out fast.
Get yourself down low.

Chorus

Verse 4
Rule Four! Don't open hot doors!
Find another way out
if a door feels hot.
Do not open it.
If it's hot, do not!

Chorus

GLOSSARY

calm—not upset or excited

practice—to do something over and over again to get it right

safety—staying away from danger

GUIDED READING ACTIVITIES

1. What are the four rules of fire safety? Write down the rules you remember without looking back in the book. Listen to the song again. How many did you know?

2. Which of the four rules seems easiest to you? Which one seems hardest? Why? Discuss the rules with the other members of your family.

3. Does your family have a fire escape plan? Find out where your outdoor meeting spot is. Draw a picture of the spot and hang it up where everyone can see it.

TO LEARN MORE

Berenstain, Mike. *The Berenstain Bears Visit the Firehouse*. New York: HarperFestival, 2016.

Herrington, Lisa M. *Fire Safety*. New York: Children's Press, 2012.

Mattern, Joanne. *How Things Work: Fire Trucks*. New York: Children's Press, 2016.

Ready, Dee. *Firefighters Help*. North Mankato, MN: Capstone, 2013.